I0023410

Frederick R. Thomas

Manual of the Discovery, Manufacture and Administration

of Nitrous Oxide

laughing gas in its relations to dental or minor surgical operations, and

particularly for the painless extraction of teeth

Frederick R. Thomas

Manual of the Discovery, Manufacture and Administration of Nitrous Oxide
*laughing gas in its relations to dental or minor surgical operations, and particularly
for the painless extraction of teeth*

ISBN/EAN: 9783337340339

Printed in Europe, USA, Canada, Australia, Japan

Cover: Foto ©Andreas Hilbeck / pixelio.de

More available books at **www.hansebooks.com**

MANUAL

OF THE

DISCOVERY, MANUFACTURE, AND ADMINISTRATION

OF

NITROUS OXIDE, OR LAUGHING GAS,

IN ITS RELATIONS TO

DENTAL OR MINOR SURGICAL OPERATIONS,

AND PARTICULARLY FOR THE

PAINLESS EXTRACTION OF TEETH.

BY

F. R. THOMAS, D.D.S.

———

PHILADELPHIA:
PUBLISHED BY S. S. WHITE.
1870.

Respectfully Dedicated

TO MY ESTEEMED FRIEND,

Z. W. SCRIVEN, M.D.

PREFACE.

THE object in writing this little work is to endeavor to supply a want long felt to exist in the literature of the subject. The necessity of a plain and practical manual on the manufacture and administration of nitrous oxide has been apparent to all who have used this agent.

The preparation of a book of this character has been undertaken by the author, under the supposition that a very extended experience with nitrous oxide would enable him to present a guide that would necessarily be productive of good results.

The intention has not been to make this a strictly scientific essay. This will be manifest

1*   (5)

upon its perusal. Had such been the design, I could have entered more fully into details upon many points that are barely touched upon. Prolixity has been avoided as far as possible, in order to keep within the limits of the original design.

The endeavor has been made to give the matter in as plain and condensed a form as possible, that it may be thoroughly comprehended and appreciated by every one in our profession.

Those who seek still further information in relation to the medicinal or physiological uses of the anæsthetic under consideration, are referred to a little work entitled "Researches on Nitrous Oxide," by Geo. J. Ziegler, M.D., Philadelphia.

F. R. T.

July, 1870.

CONTENTS.

CONTENTS

NITROUS OXIDE.

NITROUS OXIDE GAS was discovered by Priestley in 1776. He procured it by exposing binoxide of nitrogen to the action of iron, which deprived it of a portion of its oxygen, and reduced it to a state of protoxide of nitrogen.

Very little was known, however, of its action and effects until Sir Humphry Davy, by a series of careful experiments, demonstrated its character. The inhalations made by himself and many others, led him to pen the prophetic paragraph, that, " as nitrous oxide in its extensive operations seems capable of destroying physical pain, it may probably be used to advantage during surgical operations in which no great effusion of blood takes place." It is said of him* that, " after a laborious series of trials, he devised the very beautiful process, now universally employed—decomposition by heat of the crystals of ammonia. Under the present name of nitrous oxide, he minutely examined and recorded its properties for the first time. He then proceeded to breathe it, and, to his rapturous delight, discovered the rapid and delectable intoxication which it produces in the majority of people. In his note-book he wrote: 'I seemed a sublime being newly created, and as possessed of new organs.'

---

* Lectures on the Atomic Theory, by Samuel Brown. Edinburgh, 1858.

*   *   *   In connection with a kind of homœopathic theory of the art of healing which he cherished at that time, the discoverer was sanguine of its useful application to medicine.   It might be the potable gold of Geber, the vivifying quintessence of the elements of Raymond Lully, the water of life of Basil Valentine, the elixir of Paracelsus, or at least some purified and attempered supporter of vitality, for its composition was almost identical in ingredients with that of the atmosphere.   *   *   After ten months of incessant labor, interrupted by an elated run in quest of squandered health to Cornwall, he published his first considerable work in the summer of 1800, 'The Researches, Chemical and Philosophical, chiefly concerning Nitrous Oxide and its Inspirations.'"

It seems remarkable that the singular
foresight that led Davy to regard the use
of nitrous oxide in surgical operations as
possible, did not induce him to extend
his researches in this direction, and thus
present to the world what has since been
demonstrated as one of the greatest
boons to suffering humanity. But it
must be remembered that the principal
operation in minor surgery, for which it
is best adapted, that of the extraction of
teeth, was then performed in a manner
that would have prevented its pre-emi-
nent advantages from being recognized.
It is well known that the time occupied
in this operation, by the use of inferior
instruments, was largely in excess of
that now required. Consequently, nitrous oxide gas would have proven inad-
equate to accomplish the desired result.

It is but another evidence in the great chain of discovery in all departments, that each one requires the more perfect complement of the collateral branches to give full effect to its own intrinsic merits. The prophetic declaration of Davy remained unfulfilled for forty-four years. During all this period the world was ignorant that a method to escape the torture of the surgeon's knife was lying dormant, awaiting some bold spirit to bring it into active use. The discovery of the anæsthetic properties of nitrous oxide, by Dr. Horace Wells, gave an impetus to experimenting with anæsthetics that led to the final introduction of ether and chloroform into general surgery.

Previous to the discovery of nitrous oxide as an anæsthetic, it had been used for the purpose of amusement in lecture-rooms. The pleasant intoxication experienced by those inhaling it produced results oftentimes ridiculous in the extreme. The most prominent thought at the moment of inhalation frequently manifested itself, and, as a result, some would resort to a speech, others to singing, fighting, etc.

It was at one of these public exhibitions, given by a traveling lecturer, Mr. Colton, in Hartford, Conn., that Dr. Horace Wells, a dentist of that city, first noticed its anæsthetic properties. The gas had been administered to several persons in the presence of the audience; one of these accidentally struck his foot, while under its influence, against a settee. On recovering from the effect of the gas, it was discovered that he had severely bruised himself. The inquiry

was made by Dr. Wells, whether he had
suffered any pain at the time the injury
was received. The answer was, that he
was not aware he had been injured until
restoration to normal condition occurred.
The natural conclusion of Dr. W. from
this incident was, that nitrous oxide
possessed anæsthetic properties, and, to
test the correctness of the theory, he de-
termined to have a tooth extracted under
its influence. Mr. Colton, the lecturer,
was invited to his office to administer
the gas, during which Dr. W. had the
operation performed. On recovering
from the effect produced by the inhalation he remarked, that he felt no more
pain than would be produced by the
prick of a pin. Dr. W. followed up the
experience thus gained by introducing a
new system of the painless extraction of

teeth; but, owing to deficient experience in the application of the anæsthetic on different subjects, he did not succeed in permanently bringing it into use. Becoming discouraged with this agent, he commenced experimenting with ether, being cognizant of the fact that the inhalation of this in a short time produced the same premonitory symptoms as nitrous oxide. From these well-established facts, Horace Wells undoubtedly deserves the credit of being the originator of anæsthesia.

This, in brief, is a synopsis of the progressive stages that led to the discovery of this great blessing to humanity. It is much to be lamented that Dr. Wells did not survive to receive the honors so richly merited, and which without doubt would have been freely

and generously awarded. While labor-
ing under a fit of despondency, he com-
mitted suicide by severing an artery.

About nineteen years of comparative
quiet on this subject succeeded, until the
previously-mentioned lecturer, Mr. G. Q.
Colton, concluded to make another attempt to bring it before the public. He
was perfectly familiar with the previous
efforts of Dr. Wells, but was not satisfied
with the results obtained. He accord-
ingly secured the services of a competent
extractor of teeth, and, by lecturing and
extensive advertising, very soon rendered
this agent more widely known, and it be-
came a popular as well as safe anæsthetic
in dental surgery. To this gentleman is
due, in simple justice, the merit of having been more successful in introducing
this great discovery of Dr. Wells. For

his untiring perseverance and persistent efforts, amid much prejudice and opposition, the full meed of praise should be freely awarded.

In order to complete the history of the introduction of nitrous oxide, it may not be inappropriate to give Faraday's experiment in liquefying and solidifying this gas. Since its introduction for anæsthetic purposes, it has been frequently suggested that a desirable end to be obtained was the reduction of its bulk to more convenient proportions. The apparatus now required to produce it is, to some, a serious objection in its administration. The difficulties attendant upon this liquefying process are well known, and render any attempt to make it practically useful doubtful, if not impossible.

Faraday* says, in regard to its lique-
faction, that "some nitrate of ammonia,
previously made as dry as could be by
partial decomposition by heat in the air,
was sealed up in a bent tube, and then
heated in one end, the other being pre-
served cool. By repeating the distilla-
tion once or twice in this way, it was
found, after examination, that very little
of the salt remained undecomposed.
The process requires care. I have had
many explosions with very strong tubes,
and at considerable risk. When the
tube is cooled, it is found to contain two
fluids, and a very compressed atmosphere. The heavier fluid, on examination, proved to be water with a little
acid and nitrous oxide in solution; the

---

* Experimental Researches in Chemistry and
Physics, by Michael Faraday, D.C.L., F.R.S.

other was nitrous oxide. It appears in a very liquid, limpid, colorless state, and so volatile that the warmth of the hand generally makes it disappear in vapor. The application of ice and salt condenses abundance of it into the liquid state again. It boils readily by the difference of temperature between 50° and 0°. It does not appear to have any tendency to solidify at —10°." In regard to obtaining it solid, he further says: " This substance was obtained *solid* by the temperature of the carbonic acid bath *in vacuo*, and appeared as a beautiful, clear, crystalline, colorless body. The temperature required for this effect must have been very nearly the lowest, perhaps about 150° below 0°. The pressure of the vapor rising from the solid nitrous oxide was less than one atmosphere. Hence it was concluded that liquid nitrous oxide could not freeze itself by evaporation at that pressure, as carbonic acid does; and this was found to be true, for when a tube containing much liquid was freely opened so as to allow evaporation down to one atmosphere, the liquid boiled and cooled itself, but remained a liquid. The cold produced by the evaporation was very great, and this was shown by putting the part of the tube containing the liquid nitrous oxide into a cold bath of carbonic acid; for the latter was like a hot bath to the former and instantly made it boil rapidly.

" I kept this substance for some weeks in a tube closed by stop-cocks and cemented caps. In that time there was no action on the bitumen of the graduation, nor on the cement of the caps;

these bodies remained perfectly unaltered."

MODE OF MANUFACTURING NITROUS OXIDE.

THE manufacture of nitrous oxide gas may be regarded as a matter of easy accomplishment by those who are constantly preparing it. But to those who have not had this experience, its manufacture is attended with many difficulties and (to them) intricate manipulations. It is my earnest desire to provide a guide to such as these, that they may be furnished with information of so plain and practical a character that they will be enabled to proceed fully prepared for the work.

Nitrous oxide has for its chemical symbol NO, and its equivalent number (22). It is formed from a salt known as nitrate of ammonia; symbol, NH_3HO NO_5.

Nitrate of ammonia is prepared by the following formula, but it can be obtained at the dental depots, or at the manufacturer's, in a prepared condition. To carbonate of ammonia, pure nitric acid is added, until neutralization is perfected, and by slow evaporation, at a moderate temperature, it becomes crystallized.

In manufacturing nitrous oxide, the fused or granulated form is used. The fused salt is prepared by melting down the crystals and allowing them to solidify by cooling into masses. The granulation is perfected by boiling and stirring the mass until it cools. The granulated I think preferable, from the facility with which it can be introduced into the retort. The fused frequently comes in

pieces so large as to render it difficult
and annoying to place them in the retort, as it necessarily requires breaking
up before this can be accomplished. The
only object gained by the use of the
fused is greater compactness, and, consequently, a larger amount of gas will be
eliminated from a given quantity.

As a preliminary step in the manufacture of this gas, the most important
thing to obtain is a convenient gasometer, an illustration of which is presented
on page 28, accompanied with full and
explicit directions in regard to its management. This form of gasometer is in
extensive use at the present time, and,
so far as I am aware, gives satisfaction.
I use a similar one in my own practice.
It is, however, not the intention to express a preference for the gasometers

made by any one manufacturer; neither
does it fall within the province of this
volume to attempt a description of the
various forms of apparatus employed for
generating the gas, only so far as to in-
vite attention to the convenience of possessing a well-made instrument. Gas
can be made in every respect as pure by
the use of a perfectly tight barrel, if
properly arranged for the purpose. A
full description of these barrel gasometers, and the readiness with which they
can be arranged, is furnished on page
33. The illustration is given to aid
those who may not have the conven-
iences for procuring a perfected instrument.

Having procured one of these gas-
holders, especial care and attention are
required in the selection of wash-bottles.

I use three of these of one gallon capacity each. In order to avoid metal tops and rubber packings, I have them manufactured to order, thus entirely avoiding the annoyance and abomination of plastering up leaky tops. All practitioners who have used nitrous oxide gas made in the old form of wash-bottles, are familiar with this trouble, always occurring after the metal and rubber packing have been acted upon by the acid in the passage of the gas. The loss of gas is also frequently very considerable.

In purifying it, it is unnecessary to use anything but a solution of the sulphate of iron in one bottle and fresh water in the other two. Some chemists recommend the use of caustic potash in addition, for the purpose of neutralizing any chlorine gas that may be present. In my judgment, however, the use of these chemicals is superfluous, as I have found by experience that the action of the gas is precisely the same, whether it is washed through those solutions, or whether it be washed through fresh water, and allowed to stand a sufficient length of time (about 5 or 6 hours) for the water in the gasometer to absorb any impurities that may have passed over with the gas.

BRIEF DESCRIPTION OF ILLUSTRATIONS AND PROCESSES ADOPTED IN MANUFAC-TURE.

FIG. 1 represents a gasometer in a position of readiness. As a preliminary step, the holder is first filled with water to within one and a half or two inches of the top; and, while this is being

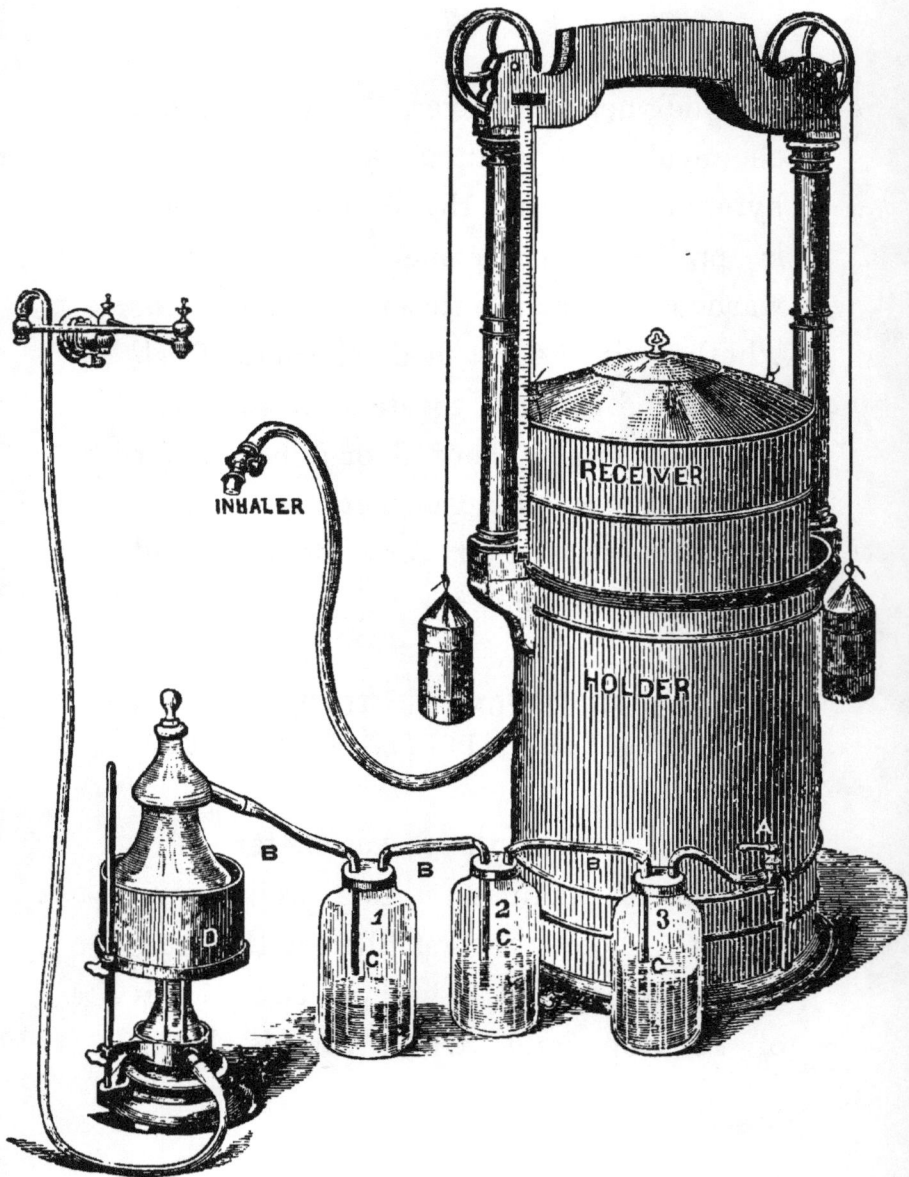

INHALER

RECEIVER

HOLDER

B

B

B

A

D

1 C

2 C

3 C

(28)

FIG. 1.

poured into the holder, take off the weights and open all the spigots, to allow the air to pass out and the receiver to remain in position. When the holder is filled, close the spigot A, and rearrange the weights. It is then ready to receive the gas. The wash-bottles should now be arranged. They are placed as represented in the cut, Nos. 1, 2, and 3, and are connected one with the other, and to the retort and gasometer, by means of rubber tubing B. The first bottle, No. 1, is placed next to the retort, and is simply used to catch the drip resulting from condensed vapor. The long pipe of bottle No. 1 must not dip under the water, for the tubing thereby becomes choked with foam, and the free passage of gas is interrupted.

Into wash-bottle No. 2 place about a

quarter of a pound of the sulphate of iron (copperas), and add sufficient water to cover the end of the dip-pipe C about one and a half or two inches. Into wash-bottle No. 3 it is unnecessary to place anything but fresh water, but some add caustic potash. Sufficient water should be used to allow the dip-pipe to sink about the same depth as it does in No. 2. In arranging the bottles, be certain to have the dip-pipe attachment facing the retort, as represented. When the bottles are prepared, connect them by the pieces of rubber tubing B, and to the spigot of the gasometer. If they are arranged properly, a current of air, blown into the tube intended to connect with the retort, will cause the water to bubble in the wash-bottles Nos. 2 and 3, and, if the spigot A is open, the receiver will commence to ascend. After the bottles are prepared and connected, I would advise testing them by closing the spigot of the gasometer, and blowing through the first tube again, to learn whether they are air-tight.

Now that the bottles are in readiness and properly connected, place the quantity of ammonia intended to be used into the retort. One pound will make about thirty gallons of gas. D is a stove-like arrangement, with a sand-dish on the top for holding and heating the retort. Into this sand-dish place sufficient sand to protect the retort, or the heat will crack it. Then place the retort into it, and connect with the long pipe of the first bottle by the rubber tubing, and then open the spigot of the gasometer.

Now apply the heat gradually, to avoid fracturing the retort, and closely observe the process. When the ammonia is melted, it very soon commences to boil; after which, regulate the heat to keep it quietly boiling until it is nearly all decomposed. Should it get to boiling too rapidly, take a dry cloth and raise the retort out of the sand-bath until the violent ebullition diminishes, when it can be replaced. Shut off the heat before it is quite all decomposed, as there is danger of breaking the retort. When the gas has ceased to come over, take a cloth and disconnect the retort from the tubing, and close the spigot of the gasometer. When the gas has remained in the gasometer from five to six hours, it is in a condition fit for use.

The water, and solutions contained in

the wash-bottles, should be changed after each operation, and the water in the holder about once in a month. As water will take up about its own bulk of gas, it will at first be found that the water has absorbed a portion of it.

To more clearly explain the mode of transforming a barrel into a gasometer, an illustration is here given. A good and perfectly tight oil or liquor barrel is generally selected for this purpose, and by a careful examination of the cut and accompanying chart, any one will be enabled to construct a gasometer in a short time, if such a resort is ever found necessary.

A represents an ordinary liquor barrel.

B and C are two spigots inserted in the top of the barrel B, connected with a hydrant to let in water. C is intended

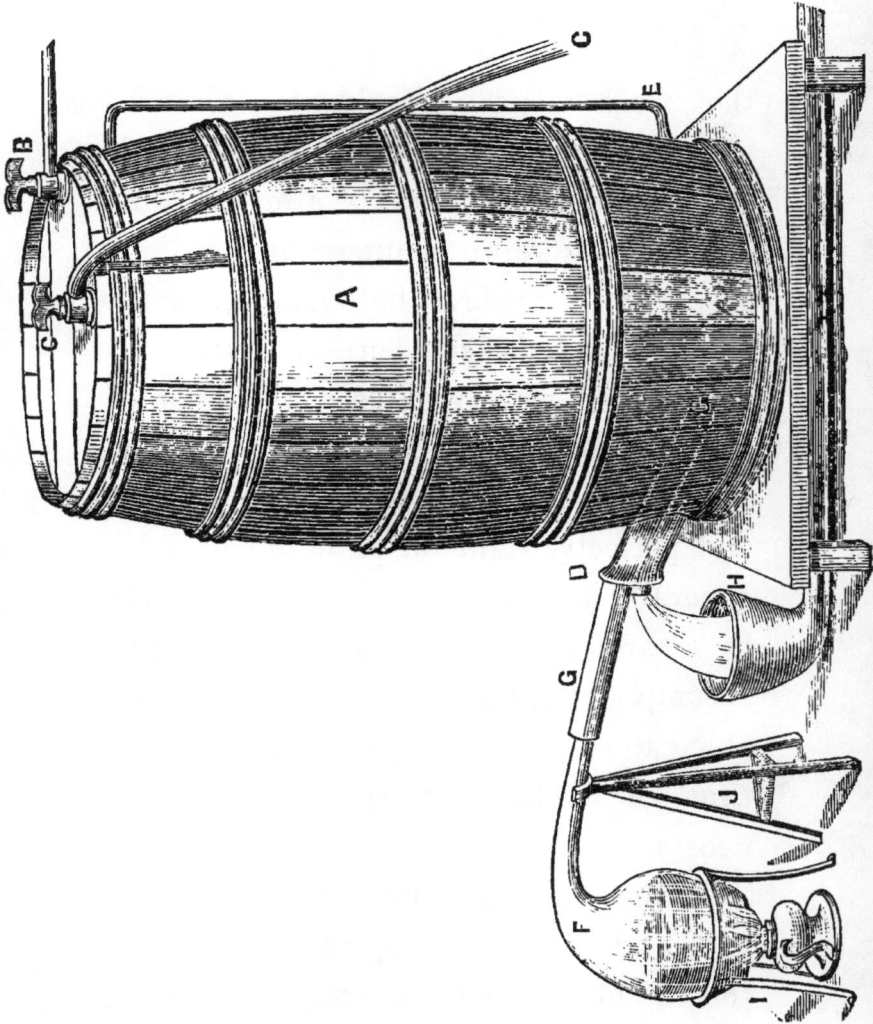

Fig. 2.

(34)

to draw off the gas, and a piece of rubber tubing is attached to C in order that it may be readily connected with the mouth-piece of the inhaling-bag. As much gas can be drawn at any time as may be required, by simply turning on the water-spigot B, and opening the other spigot C at the same time.

D is an iron tube, five or six inches in length, and about two inches in diameter. It is inserted at an angle of about thirty degrees, and has a cap to screw in to keep it perfectly tight after the gas is made. This tube is prepared of sufficient diameter to admit the rubber tubing, which is connected with the retort, to pass through and not over it. A large space must be left around it to allow the water to pass out as rapidly as the gas is generated.

E is a glass tube inserted at the side of the barrel to register the quantity of gas.

F is the retort.

G is a piece of rubber tubing, about eighteen to twenty inches long, used to connect the retort with the barrel. It is calculated to enter the barrel four or five inches.

H is a waste-basin to carry off the water.

I is the sand-bath and burner.

J is a stand to support the retort.

In manufacturing nitrous oxide in an apparatus like this, no chemicals are needed, inasmuch as it receives sufficient purification in its passage through so large a quantity of water.

- When the register indicates the barrel to be nearly full, disconnect the rubber

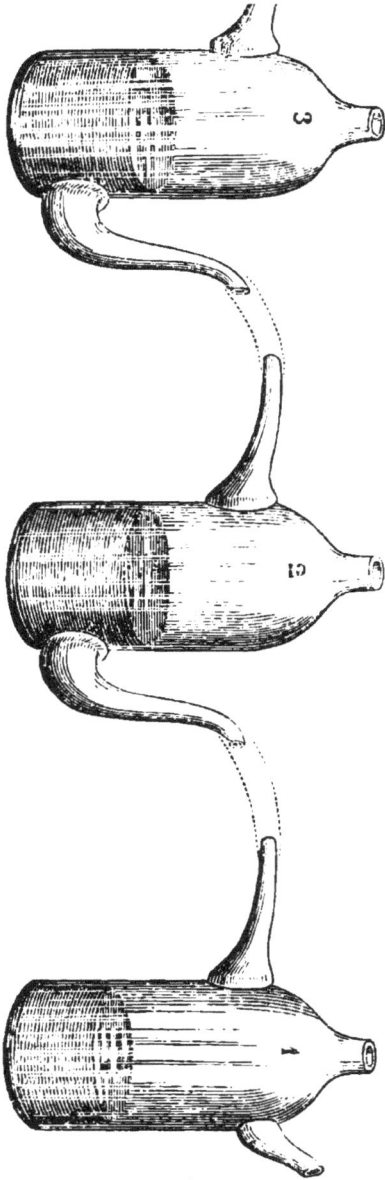

Fig. 8.

tubing from the retort, draw it from the barrel, and place a cap over the tube D; then allow the gas to stand six or seven hours before using.

Fig. 3 shows improved wash-bottles. Nos. 1, 2, and 3 are arrangements of my own. They are blown to order, and do away entirely with metal tops and rubber packing.

Fig. 4 is still another improvement, made by S. S. White. It consists of a large glass jar, with a rubber cork placed in the top in which glass tubing is passed, as represented in the cut. This is an excellent arrangement.

Fig. 4.

THE DEGENERATION OF NITROUS OXIDE.

The theory is entertained by many
that nitrous oxide will retain its potency
for any length of time; indeed, some
have promulgated the idea that it is
even better, and more agreeable and successful in its effects, after being kept for
weeks, than it is when freshly made.   I

think, however, it is a mistaken theory, and cannot be accepted for two reasons: first, that experience in its application has convinced me to the contrary; and secondly, on account of the natural affinity between water and oxygen. The fact that water absorbs large quantities of this gas is well known, and as there is no affinity between nitrogen and water, it must of necessity be the oxygen that is absorbed. The result is, that the potent constituent of the gas gradually diminishes, while its diluent, nitrogen, remains the same as when first generated. I am, therefore, confirmed in the opinion, that after nitrous oxide has been kept over four or five days it becomes very much deteriorated by the absorption and loss of oxygen. It will, therefore, require an increased quantity

over the ordinary amount to produce
anæsthesia. Indeed, I have witnessed
instances where patients had inhaled gas
kept for several days, and it seemed the
process might be continued indefinitely
without producing any impression except that of partial intoxication. I
have also had patients visit my office
directly from others, who assured me
they had inhaled unusually large quantities of gas and found it inoperative;
and they had been informed by the operator that nitrous oxide, in their case, was
inefficient. Upon the administration of
fresh gas to these, I found they were as
easily brought under its influence as
others, proving conclusively that they
must have inhaled impure gas, or that
its administration had been improperly
managed.

4*

In view, therefore, of these circumstances, I would advise all who wish to
use this agent, with uniform success, to
manufacture no more at a time than will
suffice for a period of four or five days.
By attention to this, the operator will be
saved the mortification of occasional failures. It will be found, when the gas is
properly prepared and administered, that
failure to produce proper anæsthesia is
impossible even in the most difficult subjects. I can state this emphatically, for
I have, during the last four years, operated on over fifteen thousand (15,800)
patients under its influence, and have
never met one in which complete narcosis
could not be produced.

THE ADMINISTRATION OF NITROUS OXIDE.

THE administration of nitrous oxide is, without doubt, of the highest importance of any subject that may claim consideration in this little volume. It is apparent that it is immaterial whether the operator possesses extensive acquirements of a theoretical and scientific character, or whether he is familiar with its history, medicinal or physiological effects; all will prove valueless unless he is thoroughly conversant with the many peculiarities developed, and the care and precautions necessary to success in its administration for anæsthetic purposes.

In my efforts to provide a guide for the administration of this agent, I shall endeavor to place before the reader, in a plain and practical manner, every particular concerning its manipulation, trusting thereby to be able to throw some light on a subject that, to many, is one of comparative darkness.

The importance of this must be evident to every reader, as upon a thorough knowledge of the mode of its exhibition will depend the success that will result; while, on the other hand, a want of this may lead to serious consequences. It must be borne in mind that, in the administration of this agent, we are continually brought into professional contact with the most delicate, nervous organisms; with persons who are entirely ignorant of the action of anæsthetics; with little, tender children, who are frequently too young to understand or appreciate any explanation that might be imparted to them; with persons suffering from organic diseases of every description; and, indeed, the list might be extended to all the real or imaginary difficulties that persons are subjected to. The operator should be gifted with great self-possession, and entire confidence in his skill, to enable him to meet the inquiries constantly made with intelligent and practical answers, and, by his decisive manner, inspiring a conviction of the safety of the anæsthetic and faith in the operator's ability. Patients judge of capability immediately upon presentation, and if the first impression be unfavorable, a want of confidence becomes at once established that it will often be found impossible to overcome.

In the preparation of this little guide, it is not my desire to impress upon the reader the importance of administering nitrous oxide in precisely the same manner that I have seen fit to adopt. I do, however, wish to be understood as asserting that, if the method described be strictly adhered to, the operator will find that success will crown his efforts, provided always, that he is gifted with sufficient intelligence and skill to carry it out. His efforts to relieve suffering humanity will be greeted by blessings and expressions of gratitude in profusion. Many persons outside of our profession think and believe that this branch of it is overcharged with disagreeable duties; I can but think and feel otherwise. Indeed, there are many occasions connected with its duties that are highly pleasing and gratifying, notwithstanding all that has been urged in opposition to specialties in our profession. To me there is nothing more gratifying than, after having relieved a patient of a distressingly painful and difficult tooth (without the infliction of a moment's pain), to feel the grateful clasp of the hand and listen to the sincere expressions of thankfulness that spring naturally from sudden relief from intense suffering. No, no; this is a great error, and, unless the human heart is callous, there must necessarily be a strong attachment to so humane a calling.

The endeavor will be made to impart, in a clear and succinct manner, the entire method of administering this agent, that the reader may be guided to similar satisfactory results in his manipulation.

As a preliminary step, it is absolutely

necessary to administer the gas entirely unmixed with atmospheric air. Some few persons have endeavored to promulgate the idea, that it is preferable to admit, occasionally, a portion of air while it is being administered. This is a great mistake, as all will discover who attempt its application.

Another very important item is, the judicious selection of inhalers. Indeed, the secret of many failures can be traced to the neglect of this important matter.

If the gas is administered through tubing connected with the gasometer, care must be taken to test the inhaler that is attached to it, that no doubt may exist of its being properly air-tight. There are many inhalers sold with valves so imperfectly fitted that they admit large quantities of air in at the sides, thus reducing the strength of the gas to such an extent that inhalation may proceed for a considerable time, with great waste of gas, without producing any anæsthetic influence. An impression is thereby created, both in the mind of the operator and patient, that nitrous oxide is valueless as an anæsthetic, when the sole difficulty lies in the imperfection of the inhaler. On page 76 will be found an illustration of desirable and reliable inhalers. Those used in my practice, with entire success, are similar to those represented.

It seems necessary, in view of the importance of this subject, to express an opinion upon the relative merits of a few of these instruments that have been introduced as desirable improvements. I allude more particularly to inhalers that

cover the mouth and nose. In a few isolated cases these may be used, but there
are many objections that may be urged,
in my judgment, against their employment. They are admissible when the
muscles of the face have become so contracted, from a diseased tooth, as to prevent the introduction of the mouth-
piece, or where there is difficulty in
breathing through the mouth. In administering gas to men with bearded
faces, they are comparatively worthless,
as air cannot be prevented from penetrat-
ing through the hair. When the mouth
is kept open (as it invariably should be
by a suitable prop), the face is thrown
out of natural proportion, and the same
difficulty occurs in rendering it air-tight.
Another, and, to my mind, an important
objection, is the fact that they cover the

BOSTON MEDICAL LIBRARY ASS'N. AUG 4 1891

face, thus rendering it impossible, in many instances, to know anything concerning the physiological action of the gas. Through the transparency of the mucous membrane of the lips we are better enabled to form an opinion of its action on the blood.

To those, however, who prefer to make use of the hoods, I would recommend that of Dr. G. T. Barker as the best. It is manufactured of soft rubber, and on this account is not as liable to bruise the face of restless patients.

Nitrous oxide gas may be administered in two ways, either direct from the gasometer, by means of a tube or hose, or from an ordinary six- or eight-gallon rubber-bag. The relative merit of these two modes is an important matter for consideration. I use, in my practice,

both methods, but prefer to administer
with the bag and plain inhaler without
valves. I find by experience that
patients are better satisfied with the
success of this manner of inhaling than
through the hose. This is a matter
readily understood, when the fact is comprehended that they can inhale the gas
with much greater freedom, and with
much less extra effort to obtain it. The
result is, that the suffocating feeling,
usually attendant upon the use of a
long pipe, is not complained of. The
cause of this disagreeable effect is also
obvious. When a patient is alarmed, as
the majority are when they present
themselves for this operation, they cannot or will not make an extra effort to
inhale the gas, and as this is required in
the use of the hose, there is a corre-

sponding complaint of deficiency of air.
It will also be found, upon experiment, to require more time and a larger
expenditure of gas to produce anæsthesia
in this manner than it does by means
of the inhaling-bag. All know that the
quicker the operation can be consum-
mated, the more satisfaction will be felt
and expressed by the patient. Objections have been made, by a few persons,
to the employment of the bag as a
means of administering. The inference
may be drawn from this condemnation
of its use, that their experience has been
very limited, and does not coincide with
that of practitioners whose opportunities
for observation have been varied and extended. The theory promulgated, that
it is a filthy and unhealthy practice, is
not founded on a basis of fact, unless

some operators make use of the bag without cleansing it thoroughly. The neglect of this very important and necessary operation naturally induces the conclusion that the bag is filthy and liable to produce disease. It is, therefore, advisable, after each and every case, that the bag be thoroughly rinsed. With care in this respect, it can be kept free from any deposit whatever.

A prop should invariably be placed between the teeth on the opposite side to that from which the teeth are to be removed. This should be inserted as far back as convenient, in order that it may not interfere with tightly adjusting the lips around the mouth-piece of the inhaler. These props may be made of wood, and should always have a neat string attached. The neglect of this

precaution was the occasion of a fatal
accident in this city a few years ago. It
is important that these, too, be kept perfectly clean. Thorough washing will be
required after each operation. The use
of corks as props cannot be recommended, as they are too soft, permitting
the teeth to imbed themselves to a trou-
blesome extent, and interfering with the
displacement required in extracting on
both sides of the mouth.

Everything being in readiness—the gas
prepared, props in condition for use, ap-
pliances at hand for administering, and
the patient in the chair—the operator
may proceed. The preliminary step is
to examine the mouth and the teeth to
be extracted. This is necessary, that
he may have a clear idea of what is to
be done before commencing.

Lancing is not advisable, except in a few isolated cases. It frequently occasions profuse hemorrhage, and where roots are imbedded in the gums, they are often so covered by blood as to be entirely lost to sight. The gums are also more liable to be lacerated in the attempt to feel for the roots than they would be by the use, without lancing, of properly-shaped alveolar forceps. Nausea may also be induced by the amount of blood swallowed. In my judgment, lancing is a superfluous operation to those thoroughly familiar with the use of forceps.

The mouth having been carefully examined, an assistant should stand at the left side of the chair with the bag charged with gas. The necessity of having an assistant to hold the mouth-piece, and in readiness to quiet patients in the event of their proving restless, is admitted by all who have attempted the administration of this gas, or of any other anæsthetic, inasmuch as restlessness frequently occurs during complete insensibility to pain.

The prop, before referred to, is now placed between the teeth on the side opposite to that from which the teeth are to be extracted. The mouth-piece of the inhaler is then inserted, and the patient instructed to close the lips tightly around the tube. The position of the operator is on the right side of the patient, with his left arm over the head, using the thumb and second finger to close the nostrils. This will permit the remaining fingers to gently press the upper lip and keep it closed on the tube.

The lower lip is gently but firmly

pressed about the tube by the fingers of the right hand. In this manner the lips can be closed so perfectly that the penetration of air and deterioration of gas is rendered impossible. The patient is then instructed to breathe back and forth into and from the bag, being requested, at the same time, to make deep and natural inspirations, with the same freedom and confidence as in breathing atmospheric air. The operator should endeavor to encourage the patient during the inhaling process, to distract the mind from the dread of the operation. This may be done by arresting the attention by interesting and cheerful conversation. Many times patients are drifted, as it were, into delightful dreams by recitations of a pleasant character as they are lapsing into insensibility. They

should be requested to concentrate their
minds upon the enjoyment of an agreeable carriage-drive, or upon a steamboat
trip, where the surrounding scenery is
grand and beautiful to contemplate; or
direct them to a pleasant visit to some
place of amusement, as a theater, an
opera, or evening party. The selection
of a theme will depend on the known or
supposed taste of the patient regarding
such matters. Thousands of patients
have assured me, on recovering con-
sciousness, that their dreams were of
such a delightful character that they felt
incensed upon the realization that their
thoughts were but pleasant hallucina-
tions. On the other hand, there is a
class of persons of such an extremely
cautious and nervous temperament that
it seems an impossibility to inspire them

with any degree of confidence as to safety or absence of unpleasant after-results. Assurances of this kind avail nothing. The effect of this fearful dread and the lack of confidence is felt throughout the system, and they are naturally led into gloomy thoughts, unpleasant visions, and all the horrid sensations and scenes peculiar to so-called nightmare. These two opposite states demonstrate the necessity of a composed, cheerful frame of mind previous to inhalation. The inference, however, must not be adopted that dreaming is a necessary consequence of the inhalation of the gas; there are very many to whom the entire time is a complete blank, remembering nothing from the commencement of the anæsthetic effect until their return to the normal condition.

After the patient has breathed the gas for a few moments, its anæsthetic influence is quickly demonstrated by the following symptoms:

First. By heavy and involuntary respirations, very much resembling the heavy or snoring sound of ordinary sleep. This is occasioned by the relaxation of the muscles of the pharynx. In some instances this heavy breathing is entirely absent, and, consequently, will not in all cases suffice as a guide.

Second. The stertorous breathing is followed by a discoloration of the blood, and the face and lips become darkened. The rapidity of the circulation is increased, and the capillaries are surcharged with discolored blood, as in approaching asphyxia. To a greater or less extent the discoloration is always

6

present, demonstrating the powerful physiological action of this agent on the circulation. This appearance is exceedingly annoying, and has led physiologists to associate it with asphyxia, as the resemblance of the symptoms to it is very marked.

Third. When narcosis has been completely produced, most patients exhibit a twitching of the entire muscular system; but this is particularly noticeable in the muscles of the face, the back of the head and neck, and also in the hands.

The combination of these symptoms furnishes the guide to complete anæsthesia. It is reasonable to expect to meet them all in the majority of cases. It is, however, a very simple matter to decide when complete insensibility to pain has been reached. An important difficulty with some dentists is, that they fail to get their patient sufficiently under its control before commencing operations, and the result is, therefore, a grand failure. I would advise careful observation of the characteristic symptoms occurring until complete anæsthesia is produced. The time occupied in effecting this result varies in different subjects, from thirty seconds to one and a half minutes, and the narcosis resulting is of about the same duration. This, to an expert extractor, is ample time to remove from three to twelve and even a larger number of teeth. It must not be supposed that this statement will hold good for all cases. The difficulties in the extraction of teeth are so many and various that no positive result can be stated. I have frequently been obliged to readminister the gas for the extraction of one tooth ; on the other hand, in several instances have removed twenty at one inhalation. Avoid all efforts to perform this operation with great rapidity. Ample time should be taken to perfect the work. It must be borne in mind that too rapid extraction frequently is the cause of serious laceration of the gums and fracturing the alveolus. This, although not a very serious matter, disfigures the jaw by deep depressions, and oftentimes renders it difficult to adjust atmospheric plates with exactness.

The effect of the gas upon the system passes away entirely in from two to three minutes after removing the inhaling-tube from the mouth and allowing fresh air to enter the lungs. There is no necessity of resorting to the restoratives usually employed after the administration of other anæsthetics. It is, indeed, quite rare that patients manifest any derangement from their normal condition. The nauseating and debilitating effects so common to other anæsthetics are avoided almost entirely by the use of this. I have administered the gas in my practice during the past year (1869) to thirty-four hundred and seventy-eight (3478) patients. I do not feel that I exaggerate when asserting that out of this large number I have had but twenty-five or thirty that exhibited any unpleasant after-effects. There are some few persons so delicately organized that the sight of blood, or a wound of any description, will produce in them vertigo, fainting, and frequently extreme nausea. There are many persons who

will swoon in ordinary conversation
if the subject of surgical operations be
broached. It is this class of patients
who constitute the majority of those
who are affected or manifest unpleasant
symptoms at the time of or subsequent
to operations. Patients in debilitated,
bilious, or dyspeptic conditions are some-
what liable to nausea; but even in such
cases it may be affirmed that sickness
and fainting are less likely to happen
when nitrous oxide is administered for
extracting teeth, than if the same operation were submitted to in the normal
condition.

In the event of nausea being super-
induced, the administration of a small
quantity of good brandy and fresh air, or
the occasional use of ammonia, will be all
that is necessary. Should hysteria occur

— a result not unusual — one or two drachms of the ammoniated tincture of valerian should be administered. This condition occurs when there has been much excitement or fright previous to inhalation.

THE POTENCY OF NITROUS OXIDE.

THE inquiries made in regard to the success or failure of this agent are so frequent, that there must be a cause for them. It is a fact well understood, that many persons will inhale the gas without any definite result, where the amount given has been largely in excess of that usually administered. This is not at all surprising, when it is remembered that there are many dentists constantly giving this anæsthetic whose knowledge of its action and administration is exceedingly limited. A great deal of mischief is thereby done, for such failures result in strengthening the prejudices of patients against its employment, because they are incapable of discriminating between incapacity and skill, and regard the imperfect results obtained as the fault of the agent. There is an unwillingness to believe that a more competent person might entirely change the result. As remarked on a previous page, it is of almost daily occurrence to have patients come to my office after having failed to receive benefit elsewhere. The efforts to overcome prejudices thus engendered and secure a second trial are attended with great difficulty. The failure of the first attempt convinced them that it possessed no anæsthetic properties of value. Questioning them always resulted in about the same answers, the substance of which was, that " I called on Doctor So-and-so for the purpose of having a tooth removed under the influence of the gas. Its administration failed to give the anticipated release from the pain in extraction. The time spent and the amount of gas consumed were largely in excess of that anticipated. I was finally informed by the operator that I was one of those peculiarly-organized persons on whom nitrous oxide would always prove ineffectual as an anæsthetic; that I must either resort to a more powerful agent, or else submit to the operation without the use of anything of this character." The assertion is very common that pain is as severely felt with as without this agent.

To overcome this difficulty, it is only necessary to make use of gas that has not been kept too long over water, and to observe carefully that in its administration all admixture of atmospheric air is entirely avoided. With these conditions carefully attended to, it seems to me impossible to fail in producing entire insensibility; and I have never met a case in which complete narcosis could not be produced. In all cases of failure that have subsequently come under my care, I have found that a proper application of the gas produced equally good results, and the patients were as readily affected as others. This proves, in my judgment, that the fault did not inhere in the gas, but could more properly be ascribed to mismanagement from a want of experience. I have never met a single instance of failure during an extensive practice of years; it is, however, true that, in a few isolated cases, the effect is quite transient, lasting but from fifteen to twenty seconds; and exceeding nervousness, caused by fear, sometimes renders the control of the patient more difficult than usual. Occasionally a patient will become restless while under the influence of the gas, owing to some delusive impression or terrifying dream, but by the aid of an assistant all such cases can be successfully operated upon.

72

Fig. 5.

DESCRIPTION OF CUT, WITH BRIEF EX-
PLANATION OF MODES ADOPTED.

In order that the administration of the gas may be rendered perfectly plain, the accompanying cut has been prepared explanatory of the process.

The patient is seated as represented. All the teeth to be extracted, it is presumed, have been examined. A napkin or rubber apron is then placed before him; the importance of this must be apparent, to prevent soiling the clothing with blood. The prop is then placed between the teeth, on the side opposite to that from which the teeth are to be removed. The patient is then instructed to make a long exhalation, in order to empty the lungs as far as possible of atmospheric air. Immediately upon the

7

completion of this effort, the assistant
should place the tube in the mouth, and
the operator proceed to close the nostrils
and lips, as represented in the cut.
Then request the patient to inhale and
exhale freely through the tube. As
soon as this is performed regularly, his
mind should be diverted as much as
possible from the operation by encour-
aging and cheerful conversation. Snoring or heavy breathing will be perceived
after a few inhalations, followed by a
change of color and twitching of the
muscles. When three or four inhalations have occurred subsequent to the
appearance of these symptoms, it is time
to withdraw the tube. The assistant
should remain by the side of the patient,
so that, should restlessness occur, he may
without delay render all necessary aid.

His services are also of value to the operator in keeping the lips out of the way of the teeth or forceps in extracting. At the close of the operation, the patient's head should be inclined forward and the prop removed from between the teeth. The assistant should be prepared with a small spittoon for the use of the patient, until he has recovered sufficiently to resume control of his actions.

The instrument table should be in a convenient position near at hand. It is better that the instruments should be kept out of sight of the patient. If they are kept in a regular position in the drawer, there will be no loss of time in seeking for them; the hand will involuntarily grasp the one needed. This is a matter of very considerable importance where time is of great value, as in the administration of this agent.

FIG. 6.

FIG. 7.

FIG. 8.

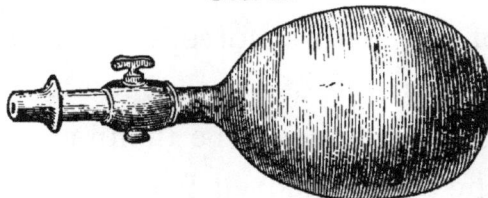

FIG. 10.

FIG. 9.

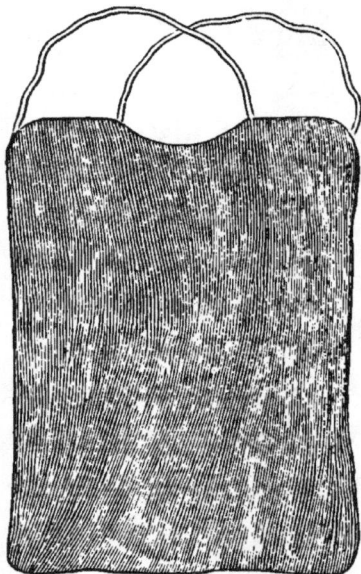

FIG. 11.

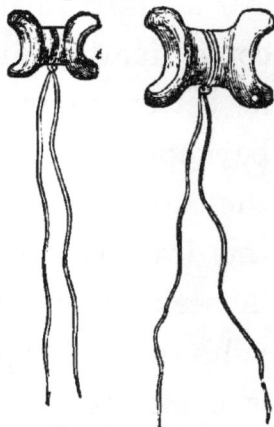

FIG. 12.

FIG. 13.

INHALERS AND ACCESSARY APPARATUS.

DESCRIPTION OF CUTS.

Fig. 6 is an inhaler made of silver-plated metal, possessing two valves, one for inhaling and the other for exhaling. This I use attached to the tubing and connected directly with the gasometer.

Fig. 7 is the plain inhaler made of vulcanized rubber, having no escape-valve. This is used with the rubber bag.

Fig. 8 is a rubber breathing-bag. It is better to have two or three different sizes, one holding five gallons for children, and one of six and eight for adults.

Fig. 9 is a soft rubber hood, designed by Dr. G. T. Barker. This can readily

7*

be placed over the inhaling-tube when needed. It is quite useful in cases where there is difficulty in breathing through the mouth. It will also be found of value where the muscles of the face have become contracted by a diseased tooth, so that the tube cannot be inserted between the teeth.

Fig. 10 is a rubber apron, and will be found very useful, as previously stated, in preventing the soiling of patients' clothing.

Fig. 11 are props to place between the teeth to keep the mouth open. They are made of wood, and should have a string attached. These props should be of several sizes, varying from three-quarters to an inch and a half in length.

Fig. 12 is a bowl of water with a

sponge in it. This is used to wash the blood from the lips and face.

FIG. 13 is a small spittoon, to hold to the mouth to catch the blood while the patient is recovering.

Some may regard these illustrations as of minor importance and superfluous; but they are, in my judgment, important, to render the entire operation perfectly intelligible to those who have had no experience in the administration of this agent.

SAFETY OF NITROUS OXIDE.

NITROUS OXIDE is, without doubt, the safest anæsthetic known for surgical operations. The time required, under its action, to produce narcosis, is much less than with any other anæsthetic in use, insensibility being successfully induced in a few moments.

There has been no other anæsthetic introduced into general practice which has not at times been injurious, and, in some instances, proved fatal. Nitrous oxide has been administered, during the past five years, to hundreds of thousands without a single instance of death resulting directly from its use. In the one or two cases reported, it was subsequently proved that death was caused by debility, and might reasonably have been expected at any moment.

To more forcibly illustrate this assertion, it may be well to state that, in the year 1869, I made a narrow escape from the charge of being accessary to the death of a patient. A lady called on me with the request that I would come to the residence of Mr. B. M. S., on Twentieth Street near Vine, to administer the gas and extract some teeth for him, at the same time stating his invalid condition and inability to go about. Being very much occupied at the time, and obliged by previous appointment to leave the city that afternoon, an engagement was made for the next morning. On returning to the city, I immediately proceeded to the residence of the gentleman. Crape on the bell-knob indicated death in the family, and on inquiry I was informed that Mr. S. had died during the night. The case is important in its relations to the safety of this agent, for a similar experience is likely to occur at any time. I feel very positive that, had the gas been administered to this gentleman on the afternoon previous, the blame would have been cast upon it, and the public would have had an additional reason for prejudice against its use. It must be remembered that life is at all times of uncertain tenure, and that from unknown causes many of our friends and acquaintances are suddenly removed in apparent health. Such dispensations of Providence cannot be avoided or evaded, and unless more satisfactory evidence against it is forthcoming, it will be hardly advisable to condemn it. It must certainly be conceded that the facts so far adduced in regard to its dangerous properties are by no means satisfactory or sufficient to warrant the abandonment of so invaluable an anæsthetic.

The result of my own experience in the administration of this gas has led me to the belief that, where there is sufficient vitality to bear the shock of extraction without the aid of an anæsthetic, it is better to administer the gas than to operate without it, always providing this is done by an experienced person. This course is not advisable for general practice, inasmuch as there exists great difficulty in discriminating who are and who are not able to bear the shock of an operation. In proof of this, the case of a clergyman is on record who visited his dentist to have a tooth extracted *without* the aid of an anæsthetic. The shock upon his nervous system was so intense that it produced congestion of the brain, which resulted in death on the following day. This is by no means an isolated case. Were it necessary, numbers might be cited to enforce the truth of the statement that nervous shock is a frequent cause of death.

Notwithstanding the foregoing remarks on the safety of this gas, it must not be inferred that no cases present in which it is contraindicated. Indeed, so positive am I of the importance of attending to these, that I am satisfied that serious consequences, in many cases, have only been prevented by watchful attention during its administration. I would therefore caution those of *limited* experience to avoid giving the gas to any but persons of known good health.

The circumstances under which experience has taught me to use extreme caution in its administration are as follows:

To persons of habitual intemperance.

In disease of the heart.

Pulmonary disease.

Excessive plethoric habit.

Debilitated dyspeptics.

Very aged people.

Children under seven years of age.

I feel confident that, if such cases be avoided, no one of ordinary skill need apprehend difficulty from nitrous oxide.

The only danger to be feared is its tendency, in exceptional cases, to suffocate. I would advise all who use it to watch closely any tendency in this direction, and, should it occur, to cease at once its administration, and allow a current of fresh air to enter the lungs. The result is a speedy return to a normal condition.

RESUSOITATION.

I SHALL not dwell at length on the subject of resuscitation, inasmuch as there appears to be but little necessity for it in connection with the administration of this agent.

As it is, however, possible that this effort may be required, it is well to be thoroughly prepared for whatever emergency may occur. I cannot, therefore, do better than to give the rules and processes so ably promulgated by Sansom in his work on chloroform :*

"It has been said that stimuli, merely directed to the heart, are useless to counteract the ill effects of chloroform. The only efficient stimulus is *respiration.*

---

* Page 160.

" The heart has been punctured with needles, galvanized, and otherwise irritated; the pneumogastrics have been stimulated; but to no purpose, further than causing a temporary pulsation. Restoration has not been accomplished by these means."

Importance of pulling the Tongue forward.

"When danger from any cause occurs in the course of chloroform administration, the tongue is apt to fall back over the aperture of the glottis.

"If the symptoms of danger are sudden and early, the tongue, instantaneously paralyzed, falling by its own weight, blocks the entrance. At the first onset of anæsthesia, the tongue, locally affected by the vapor, becomes partially insensible, and its movements are, to some extent, beyond control. In the advanced stages, it partakes of a greater amount of the general paralysis, and by its weight impedes the respiration and deepens the stertor.

"At every adverse sign, therefore, the tongue should be well drawn forward. Thus favored, the entrance of air may be induced by spontaneous inspiration; if this does not occur, it is still as important during the artificial respiration.

"The finger may be used to hook the tongue forward, or its tip may be seized with a pair of forceps—vulsellum or artery forceps being the best for the purpose. The finger and thumb covered with a handkerchief constitute probably the best means."

Methods of Artificial Respiration—Mouth-to-Mouth Insufflation.

"M. Ricord first succeeded in restoring two patients to animation by mouth-to-mouth inflation of the lungs. So, at the early period of the use of chloroform, it was hoped that the universal remedy for chloroform overaction had been discovered. The history of the cases shows more probable value in those cases in which the respiration ceases, the pulse continuing."*

Dr. Snow relates the following successful case: A patient, a lady over sixty years of age, required to have a polypus removed from the nose. She seemed to

---

* See Bickersteth, Edinburgh Monthly Journal, 1853.

be in a state of great alarm just at the time when insensibility occurred; the breathing ceased, and the pulse could not be felt. (Sympathetic paralysis—syncope.) No heart-sound could be heard. Mr. Furgusson, who was about to perform the operation, applied his mouth to that of the patient, and, by a powerful expiration, inflated her lungs. A few more inflations were made at intervals. At first the heart assumed a very rapid and feeble action; then the patient made several gasping inspirations, and soon natural breathing and pulse were re-established.* A narrow escape from a fatal result is recorded.† The sign of danger was the fact that, in the course of an operation for the removal of a tumor of the breast,

* Snow, p. 260.
† Gaz. des Hôpitaux, No. 16, 1858.

the escape of blood suddenly ceased; the action of the heart had stopped. M. Demarquay immediately practiced mouth-to-mouth inflation of the lungs. After the lapse of three minutes a feeble pulse returned; in six or seven minutes danger was over.

"These cases are enough to show that this ready means is most important for overcoming the signs of danger in chloroform narcotism. Mouth-to-mouth insufflation is of especial importance when the adverse signs are sudden and early; whenever, as I have before said, there is sudden sympathetic paralysis. In cases in which elimination has to be carried further, where there is a profounder influence of the chloroform upon the system, a method which is capable of greater protraction is indicated."

I might continue this subject and give full descriptions of the various modes adopted to effect resuscitation; but I do not deem it necessary, inasmuch as I regard mouth-to-mouth insufflation as the best remedy in the event of such a calamity occurring.

THE PHYSIOLOGICAL ACTION OF NITROUS OXIDE.

THE amount of positive information arrived at in regard to the physiological action of this agent in the progress of investigation is, so far, exceedingly limited. That which has been promulgated abounds largely in theorizing upon a limited number of facts. It seems strange that so many discordant and directly antagonistic views should be entertained upon a subject so extensively studied as this has been since the time of Sir Humphry Davy. Yet, when we consider the comparatively recent period since its physiological effects have been regarded of any importance, this contrariety of opinion finds a legitimate excuse. It is, however, none the less remarkable that effects, noticed by all observers, should be ascribed to such a variety of causes. In investigating this subject, the seeker after information must largely depend upon his own powers of analytical reasoning and close observation of cause and effect, and not too much upon the views so far promulgated by any one observer.

It is not my intention, nor would it be consistent with the object of this volume, to enter into an extended discussion of this branch of the subject; but a condensed statement of the views entertained is necessary to render it clear to the mind of the reader.

The two prominent theories advanced are, in brief:

1st. That the symptoms manifested in the administration of nitrous oxide are precisely those exhibited in the inhalation of other well-known deleterious gases, producing a condition of asphyxia.

2d. That the excess of oxygen carried to the circulation by the inhalation produces a state of overstimulation or hyperoxidation.

In illustration of the view, that narcotism is suspended oxygenation, we find a distinguished author writing as follows :*

---

* Chloroform, its Action and Administration. By Arthur Ernest Sansom, M.B., London. Lindsay & Blakiston, Philadelphia.

"Anæsthetics are agents which, when absorbed into the circulation, exert an influence upon the blood. They are shown to have the power of altering its *physical character and physical properties.* By an action upon its constituent (pro-teinous) elements, they tend to alter and, by a profounder action, to destroy its organic molecules. Its physical perfection being interfered with, its function is held in abeyance; the changes which contribute to constitute perfect life are retarded. Narcosis ensues, and is due, not to the influence of a circulating poison, but to the influence of an altered blood. * * * Narcotism (or, to speak more particularly, chloroform narcotism) is due not to a special poison 'that mounts up to the brain,' but to an altered blood. Then 'narcotism is a suspended oxygenation.'

Whatever produces, to a certain extent, insufficient aeration of the blood, produces narcosis; and whatever produces narcosis, produces, by some means or other, imperfect aeration of the blood."

Dr. W. H. Broadbent says:* "When it was suggested that the anæsthetic effects of protoxide of nitrogen were due to apnœa, and this gas was denounced as an asphyxiating agent and not a true anæsthetic, it was apparently intended to indicate a wide difference in the mode of action. There *is* a difference, but it is in the means, not in the end,—in the process, not in the result. From the fact that, in order to obtain insensibility without excitement, the nitrous oxide

---

* British Medical Journal, June, 1868, p. 620.

must be given unmixed with air, it is probable that it acts simply by preventing the access of oxygen to the nervous centres. Chloroform, which, in the proportion of 5 per cent. in the air inspired, produces anæsthesia, goes with the oxygen to the nervous centres, and obstructs the oxidation which normally occurs. In both cases the effect is due to arrest of the oxidation which yields nerve force. It is true that this explanation of the action of chloroform, and of the anæsthetics generally, originally advanced, I believe, by Dr. Snow, is repudiated by Dr. Richardson; but his objections are overthrown by a few simple experiments which I have made and hope to publish before long."

In further illustration of this, Dr.

9

Thomas W. Evans remarks :* " The theory which extensively obtains in the United States, that nitrous oxide acts upon the blood as an oxygenating agent, is quite disproved by the results of observation. The fact that nitrous oxide contains a greater proportion of oxygen than atmospheric air, is no evidence, even *a priori*, that it possesses a greater oxygenating activity. The deutoxide of nitrogen is, as compared with nitrous oxide, doubly rich in oxygen; but it is not only immediately fatal to animal life, but is even incapable of supporting combustion.

" One of the first principles of chemistry is, that in ' mixtures all the elements retain their peculiar properties;

* Physiological Action of Nitrous Oxide Gas. Dental Cosmos, June, 1869, p. 286.

in the compounds which result from a combination, each element loses the properties which characterize it, and a new body is produced.' In brief, the properties of chemical combinations can never be predicated from a knowledge of the elements which compose them."

The opposite view, that a condition of hyperoxygenation occurs in the administration of nitrous oxide, is fully set forth by Dr. Ziegler,* who, it will be seen, partially sustains this theory. He says: "Respecting the *modus operandi* of protoxide of nitrogen, there is very little doubt but what it exerts both a material and dynamic influence upon the animal

* Researches on the Medical Properties and Applications of Nitrous Oxide, Protoxide of Nitrogen, or Laughing Gas. By Geo. J. Ziegler, M.D. Philadelphia: J. B. Lippincott & Co., 1865.

organism through each of its constituents singly and conjointly; yet, notwithstanding the peculiar character of its biological effects seems to conclusively prove that they are dependent upon its constitutional elements in their separate as well as combined state, it is by some thought to act through one exclusively. Nevertheless, though it is obvious that much of its potency is derived from the oxygen, it is demonstrable that it alone is not sufficiently energetic to account for all of the phenomena resulting from the operation of nitrous oxide upon the human system, some of these being so entirely distinct from the usual action of that element as to justify the conclusion of the additional influence of the nitrogen for their production."

Further on he remarks:

"As an *anæsthetic*, protoxide of nitrogen is also unique, differing essentially from all other agents of the kind in chemical constitution, physical properties, and physiological influences, for these latter are not only chemically dissimilar, but always more or less sedative in their action upon the animal organism; whereas, the former is *ab initio* primarily and permanently stimulant, not even being followed, unless in exceptional cases, with any of that languor or depression so peculiar to the others. * * The physiological influence of nitrous oxide is, however, the reverse of this; for, instead of retarding, it, on the contrary, increases oxidation of the fluids and solids of the body, stimulates the brain and nervous system, augments general and special sensibility, excites muscular and

general contractility, accelerates molecu-
lar metamorphoses, promotes general
nutritive and vital action, invigorates
the whole system, and acts as a true
tonic."

The absence of a supply of atmospheric
air to the lungs produces what is termed
asphyxia. That this condition is a result of the non-oxidation of the blood,
there can be no doubt. It has been
demonstrated that the natural color of
the blood is dark, and that the color of
venous blood is not owing to carbonic
acid. It has been demonstrated that
carbonic acid may exist in arterial in
greater amount than in venous blood,
but normally oxygen exists in much
greater amount in the former than in
the latter. In the administration of
nitrous oxide, the lividity of the lips,

and other symptoms, indicate that under its influence the blood practically circulates as venous.

The theory that nitrous oxide possesses oxygenating powers by virtue of its oxygen, is attempted to be illustrated by the well-known fact that any substance in a state of ignition will burn with increased brilliancy when immersed in it. That this reasoning is fallacious, follows from the fact that the high temperature of the body so immersed produces decomposition of the nitrous oxide. "In no case does it enter into combination. It is decomposed by the high temperature of the burning body, and the affinity of this last for oxygen, and the combustion is maintained by means of the oxygen, which is thus disengaged. After the process is completed, the nitrogen of the nitrous oxide remains free."*

Atmospheric air contains about one-fifth part of oxygen to four-fifths of nitrogen, while nitrous oxide contains in its combination one part of each of its constituents, showing the amount of oxygen in the latter to be largely in excess. The fact that oxygen is a supporter of combustion, and possesses powerful vitalizing influences, and that nitrogen is a non-sustainer of life, has induced the belief that the term hyperoxidation is the one most appropriate to use in explaining the attendant phenomena. But when it is remembered that the same results are obtained from long-continued inhalation of oxygen as from that of

* Kane's Chemistry. 1846.

other deleterious gases, it is safe to assert
that asphyxia is the only term by which
to clearly express the conditions presented. It is found that the administration of this gas results in a progressively
increased change in the color of the
blood, growing darker and darker as inhalation continues, accompanied by increased lividity, indicating approaching
asphyxia. Upon the cessation of the inhalation of the gas and the admission of
fresh air to the lungs, the circulation as
rapidly changes in color, and the indi-
vidual is restored to a normal condition.
If this practical illustration of its effects
proves anything, it is that nitrous oxide
cannot be administered for any length
of time beyond the point of complete
anæsthesia, without resulting in death by
suffocation. I doubt, however, that this

result would be accomplished with the same degree of rapidity as has been demonstrated to occur in lower animals. In these the power of vital resistance to abnormal conditions is not equal to that of man.

If, therefore, suffocation may ensue, as before intimated, from an excess of oxygen, inhalation of carbonic acid gas into the lungs, drowning, hanging, or by any means through which the supply of atmospheric air is cut off, it follows that the similar condition of the blood presented in these cases to that under the administration of nitrous oxide, justifies the conclusion arrived at of its being an asphyxiated condition. The opinion has been entertained by some that nitrous oxide undergoes a rapid change into carbonic acid gas imme-

diately subsequent to inhalation, and
that it is owing to this chemical change
that the dark color is produced. In my
judgment, this theory cannot be sus-
tained in opposition to the results so
abundantly manifest in the administration of this agent.

The gas is first inhaled into the lungs,
then absorbed by the blood, carried to
the heart, and thence to the brain and
extremities. The circulation of the
blood requires about thirty seconds to
complete the circuit. In about this
period the effects of the gas become dis-
cernible and the cerebral hemispheres
affected. In regard to how or why this
anæsthetic acts upon the nerve centres
in the manner exhibited, remains, like
many others in physiology, a question
that it will require time and careful ob-

servation to elucidate. It is to be hoped that those best qualified for this work will continue their labors in this direction, until theory is supplanted by *absolute knowledge*.

ADMINISTRATION OF NITROUS OXIDE FOR OPERATIONS IN GENERAL SURGERY.

WHEN nitrous oxide gas is administered for protracted operations in general surgery, the effect can be continued for a considerable length of time. It is administered in the same manner as previously directed, excepting that, after the patient has become entirely insensible, the tube should be withdrawn, and every few moments the lungs allowed to become inflated with atmospheric air. Proceeding carefully in this manner, the patient may be retained under its influence for an extended period. I have administered this agent a number of times at medical clinics in our colleges and city hospitals, also in a large number of minor operations at the surgeon's office and at private residences, and in all of them have been very successful. I may, however, add that, in my judgment, ether and chloroform are preferable for protracted operations.

SUGGESTIONS IN REGARD TO EXTRACTION.

A VERY important and indispensable aid in the use of nitrous oxide will be found in the judicious selection of forceps and elevators. The extremely awkward instruments used by some dentists render it by no means surprising that they meet

10

with limited success in extracting. In consequence of this want of skill, they condemn the anæsthetic, when the blame should be credited to their lack of dexterity, as well as to the form of the instrument used.

The time allowed by this anæsthetic is said to be too short to effect anything, when the truth is that the period of complete narcosis is sufficient to admit of the extraction of a number of ordinary teeth. This fact has been already referred to in a preceding page. It must be fully understood that, in the selection of instruments, due regard should be had to convenience of shape as well as adaptation for the purpose. If this plain requirement is neglected, much time will be wasted in awkward manipulation.

It is doubtless well understood that the entire time devoted to anæsthesia must be under the control of the operator; otherwise the patient may recover before he is prepared to commence. It is therefore necessary to employ forms of instruments that will admit of operations on either jaw, without the necessity of the operator moving from one side of the chair to the other.

Dentists are liable to make the very great error of providing themselves with a large number and variety of forms of instruments. Indeed, a few seem to take special pride in arranging and exhibiting extracting instruments, under the mistaken idea that it will inspire confidence in them, and foster the opinion that they are thoroughly equipped for all emergencies. Now, it is eminently proper, and the part of wisdom, to be prepared with a sufficient supply of instruments to complete an outfit in any branch of surgery or mechanism; but there is a possibility of extending such supplies beyond a judicious limit. Where so large a stock exists to select from, the tendency is to confuse the operator in his selection. Where many teeth are to be extracted, the waste of time required in the adaptation of forceps to each particular tooth is equal to that spent in operating. This is a very common error, and one that will materially affect their success in combating the many difficulties experienced in extracting with this agent.

I would suggest that, in the selection of forceps, care should be taken to secure those that will permit the operator to always stand on the right side of his

patient, and not in front. The advantage
of this position over any other must be
obvious upon reflection. When standing
at the right of the patient, the operator
has the free use of his left arm to steady
the head, and also the use of his fingers
to draw the lips out of the way of the
forceps, as represented in the cuts, Figs.
14 and 15. His right arm gains considerable force and strength by its being
braced and steadied against the breast,
and additional power is received from
the muscles of the chest and shoulder,
increasing the ability to hold the patient
firmly in the chair.

By cuts and descriptions here presented, I have endeavored to impart a
few suggestions that may be of material
advantage to many, as they perfectly
harmonize with the previously described

10*

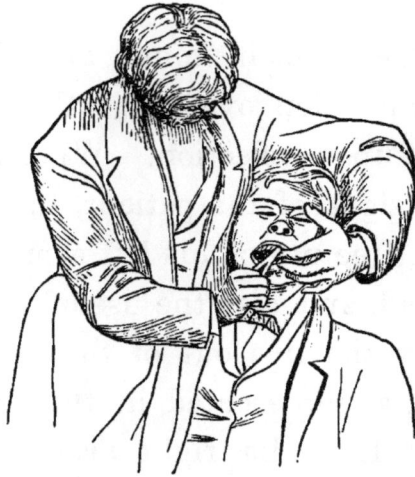

Fig. 14.

Fig. 15.

(114)

working position. As a preliminary step
in extracting, I would urge every one to
sink the beak of the forceps, in all cases,
deep under the gum, before clasping the
tooth. The neglect of this vital, practical point is the principal cause of the
breaking off the crowns of teeth by timid
operators. Therefore do not fear to in-
sert deeply, it being much better to remove a portion of the alveolar process
than to allow any of the root to remain
to suppurate.

FORCEPS USED IN MY OWN PRACTICE UPON THE TEETH OF THE SUPERIOR MAXILLA.

FIG. 16 represents forceps used for the
superior molar teeth of either side. I
would suggest the clasping of the forceps
in the manner represented in Fig. 14.
In using forceps in extracting teeth,

Fig. 16.

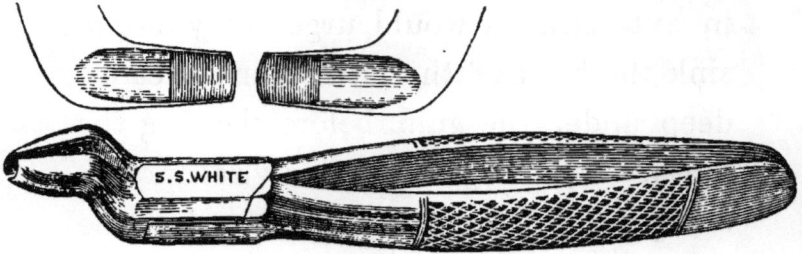

avoid clasping it with the palm of the
hand turned upward, as an equal amount
of force cannot be applied.

Fig. 17 is known as "Parmly's bay-
onet forceps," and is adapted for use on

Fig. 17.

broken-down or deeply-decayed roots of
molar teeth.   It is also well suited for

the bicuspid teeth and roots on either side of the superior maxilla.

Fig. 18.

FIG. 18 is also an alveolar forceps, and is known as "Parmly's straight beak." It is used to extract the six anterior teeth and roots. I consider it superior to the broad file - cut beaks for this purpose, inasmuch as these teeth require to be turned slightly as they are drawn; and in attempting to rotate a tooth with a file-cut beak, it will slide around the tooth. The danger of cutting or breaking off the crowns of teeth is avoided by the use of this instrument, provided it is properly managed.

FORCEPS USED UPON THE INFERIOR MAXILLA.

FIG. 19.

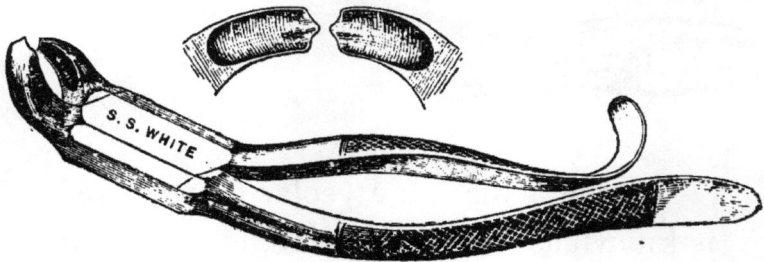

FIG. 19 is a forceps used in extracting the molar teeth on either side. Many prefer to entirely confine its use to teeth on the right, as a corresponding instrument exists for the left side. I regard this latter as superfluous. The pair described is invaluable for either position.

FIG. 20 is an alveolar forceps. It also comes in this form in pairs; but I use only that originally intended for the

FIG. 20.

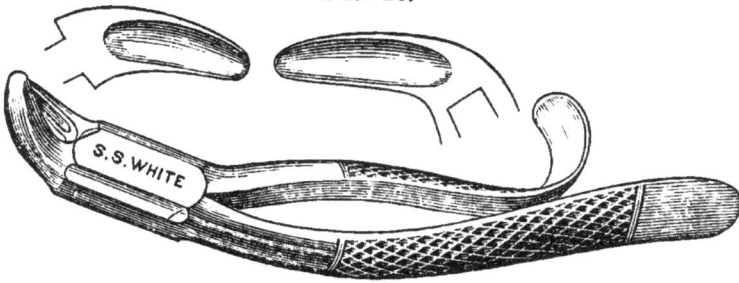

right side. It is adapted for deeply
decayed and broken molar teeth and

FIG. 21.

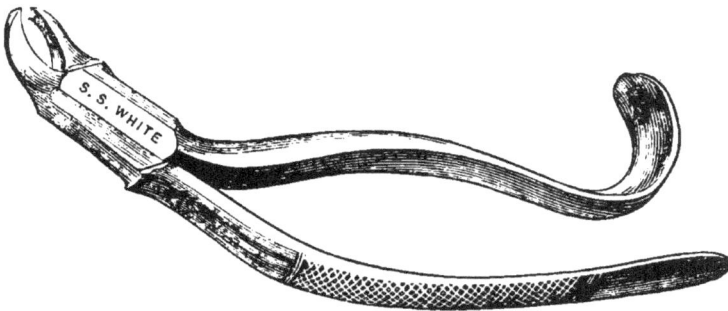

roots, and also for bicuspid teeth and
roots of either side.

FIG. 21 represents forceps used in the

extraction of the six front teeth and roots or bicuspid of the right side.

The preceding cuts represent the style of forceps employed in my practice. They will, upon trial, be found to meet all ordinary cases of extracting.

For the extraction of crowded teeth, it will be found of advantage to make use of one or two pairs with very narrow-pointed beaks, and the selection of them may be left to the judgment of the operator, in order that he may conform to the emergencies of such cases.

I make use of but three elevators. The following illustrations will sufficiently demonstrate their forms. I never employ these except for the purpose of extracting loose roots or the roots of the inferior wisdom teeth, where the alveolus is so thickened as not to admit of the

judicious cutting through of the process
with the forceps.

Fɪɢ. 22.

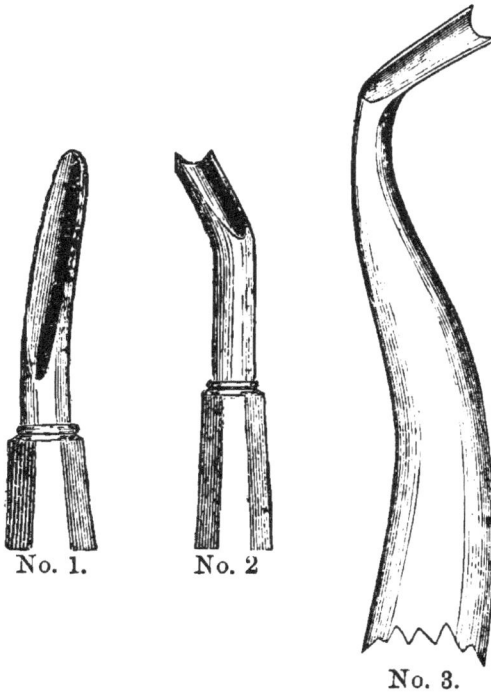

No. 1.   No. 2

No. 3.

Nos. 1 and 2 are used in different posi-
tions of the mouth in accordance with

11

judgment and convenience. No. 3 is an arrangement entirely my own. It is very convenient to extract the roots on the left side while standing on the right, and has proved a useful instrument.

In conclusion, I would suggest to dentists who use the "Cowhorn" and "Physick" Forceps, to be extremely careful in their management, as there is great danger of throwing the tooth into the pharynx, thus rendering it liable to be drawn into the opening of the larynx, and thereby choking the patient.

NITROUS OXIDE GAS APPARATUS.

*Illustrated on page 28.

Complete Apparatus, 40 gallons' capacity $71 50
"   "   50   "   " 75 00
Boxing (additional) 2 50

*The new Wash Bottles (No. 1) on following page, are substituted for those shown in the cut, and the Eagle Gas Stove in place of the Sand Bath.

SAMUEL S. WHITE.

RETORTS.

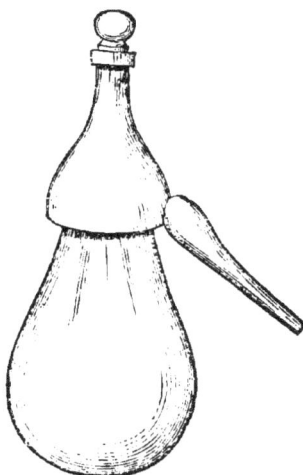

Tubulated Retorts, flint glass, half-gallon, of shape illustrated. Made expressly for our sales, and highly spoken of by those who have used them for manufacturing Nitrous Oxide.

Price $1 50

SAMUEL S. WHITE.

11*

WASH BOTTLES.

No. 1.   No. 2.

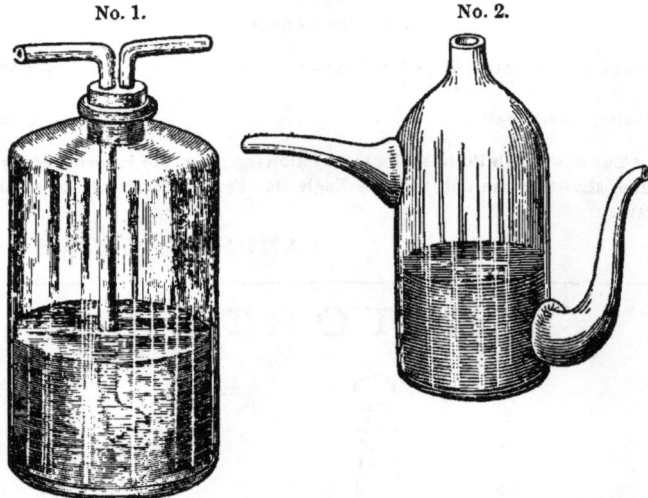

The cuts represent two varieties of Wash Bottles for the manufacture
of Nitrous Oxide Gas. No. 1, with perforated Rubber Cork and Glass
Tubes bent at right angles; the long tube pierced with small holes at
the bottom. to compel the breaking up of the gas, and so insure its
more thorough washing. No. 2, Dr. F. R. Thomas' pattern.

No. 1	each	$2 50
No. 2	"	2 00

SAMUEL S. WHITE.

FUSED NITRATE OF AMMONIA.

We ask especial attention of the profession to this article, manufactured expressly for our sales, and which we can commend for its
purity.

Price, in 1 lb. paper	60 cents per lb.
" " 5 " boxes	60 " " "
" " 10 " "	60 " " "
" " 25 and 50 lb. boxes	50 " " "

GRANULATED AMMONIA AT THE SAME PRICES.

We will furnish Nitrate of Ammonia or the cheaper kinds, when
especially ordered, at the market prices; but as much of that offered
contains free nitric acid, and is otherwise impure, we do not keep it on
hand.

SAMUEL S. WHITE.

WILLSON'S AUTOMATIC INHALERS.

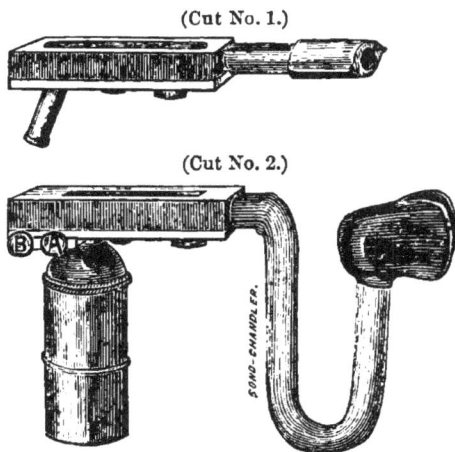

(Cut No. 1.)

(Cut No. 2.)

SONO-CHANDLER.

The valves of these instruments, at the orifices for inhaling and exhaling, are attached to bars poised upon a fulcrum, so that the slightest breath will open the former FULLY, close the latter perfectly, and vice versa.

An air passage is provided, having a valve held open by a spring; — when the instrument is at rest, this spring also closes the inhaling and exhaling valves.

On commencing administration, the patient is not told to "empty the lungs," but to breathe NATURALLY. At the proper time the assistant presses the spring, and the patient calmly passes into insensibility, much more uniformly both with regard to the length of time occupied and the quantity of material consumed, than when gravity or suction valves are used, because of the inaccuracy of their work.

Cut No. 1 represents the Inhaler used for Gas; having the mouth-piece movable.

Cut No. 2, that for Ether or Chloroform; their admixture with air, by the use of this Inhaler, is under the control of the operator; the desired percentage of vapor being regulated by marked slides, attached to screws.

Price of the Gas Inhaler $10 00
    "   " Vapor " with two sizes of Face-piece (Goodwillie's) 15 00

SAMUEL S. WHITE.

DR. F. R. THOMAS' INHALER.

This inhaler is made of metal, silver-plated; has two valves—one for inhaling and the other for exhaling—sufficiently large to allow natural respiration; it also has a slide to close the inhaling valve, thus preventing the escape of gas. Entire length of the instrument, six inches. Price $10 00.

SAMUEL S. WHITE.

GOODWILLIE'S PATENT INHALER.

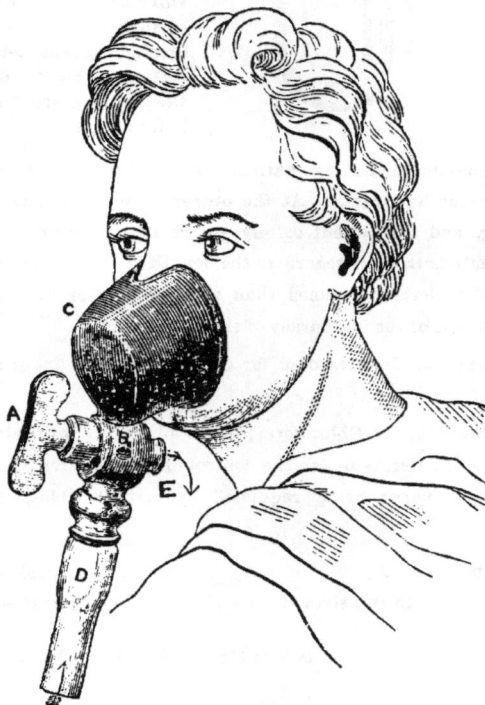

DESCRIPTION OF INHALER. — A Faucet, containing the Valves, and revolving quarter of a circle. B, Fresh Air Valve. C, Face-piece. D, Inhalation Valve. E, Exhalation Valve.

As the Face-piece covers both the mouth and nostrils, the patient may breathe through either, and by the arrangement of the Valves the breath is thrown off by the Exhalation Valve (E), and danger of asphyxia avoided. It is made of Hard Rubber, nicely finished, with two Face-pieces of different sizes. Price, in box, $10 00.

SAMUEL S. WHITE.

NITROUS OXIDE GAS INHALER.

OUR OWN DESIGN.

The Face-piece, which is designed to cover both mouth and nostrils, is made of Metal, Silver-plated; the Stop-cock is of Hard Rubber. Two Valves—one for inhaling and the other for exhaling—are affixed to the Mouth-piece, sufficiently large to allow natural respiration. Entire length of the Instrument nine inches.

Price, inclosed in a neat Box $8 00

SAMUEL S. WHITE.

HARD-RUBBER INHALER.

With two flexible Rubber Valves in Stop-cock (one opening inward to allow the gas to pass in at inspiration, which closes by the force of the expiration). Silver-plated Cap at end of Stop-cock with orifice, as shown in cut, to allow the escape of the expirations.

Price $4 00
Inhaler without Valve, price 2 00
Flexible Rubber Hood, to cover mouth and nostrils, price . . 1 00

SAMUEL S. WHITE.

NOSE COMPRESS.
INTRODUCED BY DR. S. S. NONES.

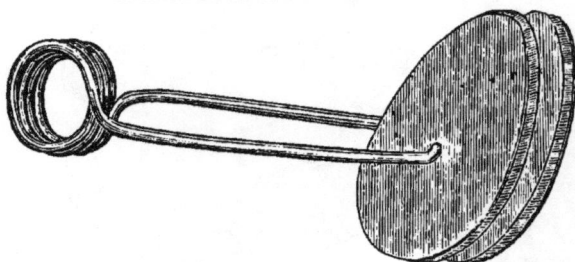

Convenient for the administering of Gas, where the Inhaler used is without a Face-piece.

Price . . . . 50 cents.

SAMUEL S. WHITE.

RUBBER TUBING.

1/4 inch, inside measure	per foot	$0	16
3/8 " "	"		20
1/2 " "	"		24
5/8 " "	"		28
3/4 " "	"		34
1 " "	"		41

The above prices are for 6 and 12 feet lengths. In less quantities, 4 cents per foot extra.

RUBBER GAS BAGS, OVAL.

5 Gallons	. . . .	4	25
6 "	. . . .	5	25
7 "	. . . .	6	25
8 "	. . . .	7	00
9 "	. . . .	8	50
10 "	. . . .	9	50

RUBBER GASOMETERS, SQUARE.

18 by 24 inches	. . . .	6	00
20 by 30 "	. . . .	8	00
24 by 30 "	. . . .	10	00
30 by 40 "	. . . .	12	00

SAMUEL S. WHITE.

PHÉNOL SODIQUE.

This valuable preparation is confidently recommended to the profession as a prompt and reliable Hæmostatic, Antiseptic, Disinfectant, and Astringent.

For hemorrhage following extraction it is preferred to preparations of iron, being entirely free from any escharotic or irritating qualities, and sedative and antiphlogistic in its action. It gives almost magical relief to the after-pains of extraction, and prevents subsequent soreness of the gums.

Its use is indicated: As a wash for the mouth in cases of diseased gums, aphthous conditions, and to disinfect an offensive breath; as a gargle in throat affections, as in scarlatina, diphtheria, etc.; in fetid discharges from the ear, in ozæna, in affections of the antrum, etc. etc. etc.

Dr. M. P. Linton says of it:

"I have at length begun to regard it as one of the professional essentials, and feel quite free to say that I know of but few articles in the whole Materia Medica that have a wider or more important range of application, and none perhaps that has so rarely disappointed my just and reasonable expectations. . . . I presume there are but few intelligent dentists, once becoming fairly acquainted with its many and valuable properties, who would ever after willingly consent to be without it ready at their hand."

In 8 oz. bottles, with directions . . . . . . 50 cents.

SAMUEL S. WHITE.

DENTAL CATALOGUE,

OF 226 PAGES OCTAVO,

CONTAINING

NEARLY 1000 ILLUSTRATIONS.

It is printed on fine paper, neatly bound, and is a

COMPLETE DIRECTORY TO THE DENTIST IN EACH DEPART- MENT OF HIS PROFESSION.

Any Dentist, or Dealer in Dental Goods, who has not already received a copy, can obtain one, free of expense, upon application. Let the name of town, county, and State, and the name of the applicant, be written distinctly.

SAMUEL S. WHITE.

CHEMICAL ESSAYS:

A COLLECTION OF CHEMICAL ESSAYS IN REFERENCE TO DENTAL SURGERY.

By GEORGE WATT, M.D., D.D.S.,

PROFESSOR OF PATHOLOGY AND THERAPEUTICS, LATE PROFESSOR OF CHEM-
ISTRY AND METALLURGY IN THE OHIO COLLEGE OF
DENTAL SURGERY, ETC.

It is a handsome 12mo volume, of 260 pages. Price $2 00.

SAMUEL S. WHITE.

DENTAL MATERIA MEDICA.

By JAMES W. WHITE.

A 12mo volume of 108 pages. Printed on fine tinted Paper. A useful Manual for the Office and Laboratory.

Paper cover $0 50
Bound in cloth 1 00

SAMUEL S. WHITE.

www.ingramcontent.com/pod-product-compliance
Lightning Source LLC
Chambersburg PA
CBHW030612270326
41927CB00007B/1136